T0365723

Twelve Days of Christmas

A mini-memoir by an erstwhile Christian

Order this book online at www.trafford.com
or email orders@trafford.com

Most Trafford titles are also available at major online book retailers.

Print information available on the last page.

ISBN: 978-1-4120-8987-6 (sc)

Trafford rev. 06/04/2021

North America & international
toll-free: 844-688-6899 (USA & Canada)
fax: 812 355 4082

Author's Note

*W*hen first I picked up my pen to record these memories of Christmases past it was with no conscious agenda. I simply wanted to pluck them from the attic of my brain where they had lain so long unattended. What might they reveal? Was I subconsciously hoping for some kind of Scroogeian epiphany? Perhaps. One thing I learned beyond all doubt: There is a great deal more in the attic than I remember putting there. I cannot swear that what I have written here is exactly as it all happened, only that this is what I remember.

J.P.

CONTENTS

DAY   PAGE

One   The Old Brown 'At   11

Two   No Lyin'   17

Three   Jiggerman   23

Four   The Demise of Santa   29

Five   Forgiven But Not Forgotten   37

Six   Great Expectations   45

Seven   "...A Lovely Light"   55

Eight   Only God   65

Nine   Empty Nest   75

Ten   Futon & Tofu   83

Eleven   An Embarrassment of Riches   99

Twelve   "Not With a Bang..."   109

Day One

(1917)

on which a very little girl first experiences a feeling of terror

The Old Brown 'At

*H*ow far back can we remember? Surely there has been some good research in this area, but I've not done my homework. Nevertheless I am going to tell you about something I distinctly remember that happened before I learned to talk.

At that time of my life I lived with my father, my mother, and my brother in a snug little house that seemed to me to be just right for our family: a kitchen, a living room, and one bedroom for each of us. Mine was the tiny corner bedroom on the shady side of the house, the one with the ladder that led up to the garret. At a certain time every afternoon either my mother or one of the other ladies who sometimes took charge of things carried me up the back stairway and bedded me down in my crib. There I stayed, happy as a clam, watching the shadows on the window shades or scanning the bright flowers on the cretonne draperies until I fell asleep – always in anticipation of the BEST time of the day, when my father came to wake me up. Quite often I wasn't really asleep when he arrived, but I pretended. He laughed and called me possum, tickled my toes, sat me on his shoulders and carried me down to supper.

Occasionally my father couldn't come and that was always disappointing but not upsetting because I knew he would be back on schedule the next day. Thus it was that I wasn't too surprised one evening when I became aware of my mother's presence in the dark room. She seemed to be moving more quickly than usual, and talking more loudly, as she scooped me up in her arms and rushed toward the front stairway. Then I heard other voices. When we reached the living room I saw several people laughing and shouting. Someone was trying to make a small tree stand up on a table. There was a bright fire in the fireplace and I noticed that my highchair had been brought in from the kitchen and placed in front of it. Once I was securely strapped in I looked around at the people. They were all familiar, all friends; people I would later learn to call Grandpa and Uncle Arthur, Aunt Jennie, Cousin Bert... My father wasn't there.

After that I don't remember any sequence of events – when or what I was fed, how the tree got trimmed, whether or not there was any exchange of presents... I do remember that there was dancing, lots of dancing – though whether the music for it emanated from the Victorola or some other source I cannot tell. Maybe my mother played the piano, though it seems to me now that she was one of the dancers.

What I do remember is that in the midst of all the revelry the front door opened and in walked father. As was his wont he went directly to my mother, embraced her and kissed her on the forehead. Then he took off his coat and overshoes and joined the party. In a very short time he became the center of attention for he was singing a song that seemed to amuse everyone – something about an old brown hat, only he said "'at". (Have I mentioned that my father was an Englishman?) Of course I did not fathom the meaning of the lyrics, but I knew he was making everybody laugh, and that made me feel very proud. Whether they hollered "Encore!" or "Sing it again, Ray" I'll never know, yet the singing and the laughing continued and the feeling of pride seemed to swell within me. I twisted around in my chair to catch my mother's attention to make sure she was enjoying the fun.

What I saw was so frightening I have never been able to forget it. She was looking at my father in such a strange way: Her eyes were wide open and glassy, her lips pulled back and skewed, gargoyle-fashion, her fingers fisted. I tried to scream but no sound came; I could scarcely breathe. There was a hard lump in my chest, as though I had swallowed a big stone. I felt icy water trickling over my shoulders and down my back.

I put my head down on the tray of my chair and played possum. That's all I remember.

Day Two

(1918)

*on which the same little girl is piqued
almost to rage*

No Lyin'

*W*hatever mayhem my mother's grimace portended seems not to have materialized, at least not within my awareness. Life after Christmas was very much like life before Christmas: peaceful, pleasant, and above all, orderly. Father went to work, Buddy went to school, Mother and I stayed home and did what had to be done. I quickly learned to chatter and make my thoughts understood, though not perfectly as you soon shall see.

I followed my mother around from room to room as she did her chores, gradually gaining permission to participate in all her wondrous activities. When we dusted the living room, my share was the piano stool, table legs and base boards. When we cooked, one of my tasks was to put the salt in the water, always the exact amount as measured out into my tiny hand. Wash day was the most exciting. Both stationary tubs in the kitchen were filled with water: one soapy, one clear. The washboard went into the soapy one and I stood on a stool and watched while mother scrubbed. "Let me, let me!" I was given a sock, a collar or a handkerchief. When scrubbing and rinsing were all completed we went out into the back yard and hung things on the line. Even in winter, if the day was fair, the clothes would be flapping in the wind before noon.

Perhaps this is a good time to mention that all this happened long before the age of consumerism. There was a Santa, of course, there has always been a Santa, but he was leaner and carried a smaller pack than the Santa we know today. He brought just one gift to each child: Something that had been asked for if possible, but if not possible, then some other pretty or useful thing in its stead.

With so much to learn and so many chores, the days and months passed quickly. Soon another Christmas season was approaching and this time I was privy to some conversations that enlightened me somewhat about the rites of that holy day. I was still taking my afternoon nap, still enjoying the pleasure of being awakened by my father. One evening when he came into my room he said, "When I go to work tomorrow I might see Santa downtown. If I do, what shall I tell him you would like him to bring you for a present?"

"A lion," I answered, without hesitation. I had been expecting the question, wishing for it.

"What kind of lion?"

"Just a regular one. Nothing special." It occurred to me that a special Christmas lion might come in red or green and that would never do.

Father was completely nonplussed. As far as he knew there had been no lions in my life. We'd had no trip to the zoo; that came much later. There were picture books around. Buddy had lots of picture books. Perhaps one of them was about lions. And then, of course, there were those little boxes of animal crackers the children were so fond of. Not-to-worry, Mother would know what to do. Mother always knew.

Since we were a family of night people, we always celebrated Christmas on the Eve. (None of your frantic early morning risings for us, thank you.) The much-touted Eve arrived and after an early supper Mother ushered us into the living room which had been magically transformed into a fairyland. A large tree, bearing the most wonderful red, green, and golden fruits and dripping with silver icicles was growing right out of the floor. (Quite a fellow, that Santa!) Gifts were spread beneath it and all about. There were coloring books and crayons, a slate with a piece of chalk on a string, a toy horse, a small pillow with legs – made to look like an animal – brown. A sheet of paper dolls. And, oh, a jacket for Jeanie with a real fur collar. How lovely! Let's try it on. There were sweets to eat and bright colored drinks. I especially remember the bright colors. Everyone found something to be excited about. Buddy drew pictures on the slate and wiped them off with his handkerchief. I enjoyed stroking my fur collar. Soon it was time for bed.

Mother picked up the brown pillow and thrust it under her arm, took my hand in hers, and we started up the stairs. "Do you like your lion?" she asked as we climbed.

"I didn't get a lion," I replied, somewhat wistfully.

Sensing there had been some misunderstanding, my mother questioned, "What did you want the lion for?"

Stupid question, I thought, but I answered it anyway, with a bit of pique, bordering on rage. "So I can HANG up my CLOTHES when we WASH. Your lion is too UP. I need a lion of my OWN."

Day Three

(1920)

*on which our protagonist learns
all about remorse*

Jiggerman

The memory I am about to recount is not considered politically correct today. It might be expedient for me to omit it altogether, yet I feel compelled to include it because for me, each early experience represents one step in the development of my emotional repertoire. This was my first encounter with remorse.

My brother's favorite Christmas toy was his Jiggerman. I don't know where he got it. Certainly not from Santa. Probably one of the uncles. It was, basically, a tin box painted to look like a log cabin, with a minstrel character, having hinged arms and legs, attached to the roof. When you turned a key on the side of the box, and then let it go, the Jiggerman would dance on the roof and make a great clatter.

I had been told many times never to touch my brother's toys, and for the most part I didn't. Boy's things were different from girl's things, except maybe books. Even his books didn't seem very interesting. Too hard. But there was something about Jiggerman that took my fancy; I couldn't keep my eyes off him. I would ask Buddy over and over to make him dance, and Buddy seemed always willing to comply.

However, Buddy wasn't always around. Sometimes he went for a whole afternoon to play with cousin Bert. On one such occasion I found myself alone in a room with Jiggerman. I needed to see him dance. I knew what could make him do it. I tried and tried to turn the key but it would not budge. I twisted and turned the whole toy, poked it, banged it against a chair, gave it a good shake. That did it! Jiggerman fell off the roof, split into two longitudinal pieces and lay on the floor at my feet.

How could I have done such a terrible thing, when Buddy had been so generous in sharing his wondrous toy? What kind of bad witch had got inside of me to make me do it? Was there any way it could be fixed? Quickly I picked up the pieces and hid them in my cubby-hole, underneath a doll's blanket. Maybe they would put themselves together. Maybe it didn't happen. Maybe it was just a dream.

When Buddy came home it wasn't long before he asked what had happened to Jiggerman. Mother didn't know, and I was upstairs taking my nap. Instinct instructed him to invade my cubby-hole (a place forbidden to him; he had his own). He lifted the blanket, gazed on the broken pieces, decided to leave them there.

At supper table after blessing had been said and potatoes passed my brother made an announcement. "Jean broke my Jiggerman."

All six eyes turned on me. "Jean?" My mother's rising inflection demanded a response. My very first opportunity in this lifetime to tell a lie and I didn't squander it. "No, I didn't."

"Then how come the broken pieces are in your cubby-hole?"

Instantaneously I learned: one lie begets another. "I don't know. I was taking my nap."

Everyone kept looking at me; the silence was awful. Tears began to trickle down my cheeks. Soon I was sobbing with abandon. If only I could make them understand! I didn't mean to do it. It was an accident. I loved Jiggerman!

What recompense was granted my brother I've forgotten, if I ever knew. My parents were eminently fair. One thing I know for sure: there was never another Jiggerman in our house. My father, a man ahead of his time, wholeheartedly disapproved of the caricature of the minstrel – even in an era when practically everyone else we knew accepted it as just part of our national culture.

Day Four

(1921)

her first experience with disbelief

The Demise of Santa

*M*ost of the furniture in our house was second hand. Not family heirlooms, mind you, just stuff from used-furniture stores. I didn't know that, of course. It all seemed quite adequate to me. But there was one piece that stood out from all the others – a really elegant piece. That was my mother's desk. When not in use it stood tall and slender on its graceful legs, its polished blond wood reflecting the light from the windows. It took on an altogether different shape when mother turned down the writing flap and revealed all the little compartments where she kept paper, envelopes, and stamps. Whenever she sat at her desk to write a letter I would sit at the telephone table near by to practice my alphabet. I was already able to recognize my name, JEAN, when Buddy spelled it out in blocks. There was always so much to learn! Someday I would be able to write like mother, and then I would have a desk exactly like hers.

It sometimes happened that mother had to make a quick trip to the grocery store one block away to buy something she had forgotten earlier. On those few occasions she left me in the care of my brother who obviously didn't relish the job, but he didn't have any choice. One such emergency arose one December afternoon in the winter when I was five. No sooner was mother out of the door when Buddy called to me, "You wanta see what we're gettin for Christmas?"

"What do you mean?" I asked.

"Come on, I'll show you. You know about Santa? He doesn't come down the chimney. He comes before Christmas and puts the presents in the garret. Then on Christmas Mom and Dad take them down and put them under the tree. I'm pretty sure he came last night. I heard him."

"I didn't hear anything."

"You were sound asleep."

He took my hand and pulled me toward my room. I'd been in the garret a few times before, but only when Mom and Dad had lifted me up, handed me from one to the other. I was deathly afraid of the ladder. I might fall through.

"It's easy. I'll stand right behind you and hold on to you all the way. Hurry up, we don't have much time."

At length my sense of adventure was aroused and overcame my timidity. We ascended the ladder and arrived on our hands and knees on the garret floor. It was dusk but we could see shapes and gradually our eyes adjusted. I saw a miniature desk just like my mother's – well, not just like it, not the same golden color – but the shape was right.

How did Santa know I would like a desk? There was another thing: a bench with a kind of table attached. That was probably for Buddy.

"Desks," said my brother in a tone I subsequently learned expresses disgust. I think he had asked for a sled. "Let's go down. Don't tell Mom; she might get mad."

We didn't have long to keep our secret. Christmas Eve came a few nights later. The living room was again transformed into a fairyland and another beautiful tree grew out of the floor. This one had lights that went on and off. It also had on it a lot of the decorations that were on the tree the year before. My desk was there, only it had three blocks on it spelling out R-A-Y. That was

Buddy's other name, the one he used in school. My name, J-E-A-N, was spelled out in blocks on the other table-thing. I waited to see if anyone would notice the mistake. No one did.

How could Santa make such a big mistake??... Wait a minute. Those blocks were not on the presents when they were in the garret. So Mom and Dad must have put them on tonight. Mom and Dad don't make mistakes. They know who gets what. Then the desk must really be for Buddy... I wanted to cry, but I knew I mustn't. Santa would probably bring me a desk next year when I could write.

There were other toys. I got a doll in a pink tutu who stood on her toes. Buddy got a whole bagful of aggies, no two alike. Mother played the piano and there were good things to eat. All-in-all it was an O.K. Christmas.

When the holiday season was over and Buddy went back to school, his beautiful graceful desk was moved up to his room. As far as I know he never used it. My bench-and-table thing was left downstairs so I could practice my letters while mother was sewing or washing dishes. It was quite comfortable for drawing and coloring but I wasn't convinced it was really a desk until the following September when I went to school and saw a whole room full of desks just like it.

One morning, after things were back to

normal and we were dusting the living room, I asked quite casually, "Mother is there really a Santa Claus?"

Moment of truth! After a slight hesitation she broke into a beautiful smile and hugged me. "Daddy and Mommy are your Santa Claus, Sweetheart. We love you very, very much. We like to give you surprises."

Surprises, indeed!

Santa was dead, not to be reincarnated until my younger sister and brother, yet to come, reached the age of believing.

Day Five

(1922)

rejection, hurt feelings, embarrassment
– they do not go away

Forgiven But Not Forgotten

A number of momentous events transpired before the onset of the next holiday season. Not the least of these was that two days before my sixth birthday my mother brought forth a pair of twins, a girl and a boy. Needless to say, my life changed dramatically. My mother's life must have changed even more dramatically, I should think, yet five months and five days after the event she would be found in her little kitchen preparing a lavish Christmas feast for her father and all her siblings, just as she had done every year since her marriage.

Grandpa and Aunt Jennie arrived first. Jennie

was my mother's only sister, many many years her junior. She came sporting a sparkling clasp in her hair, tortoise shell with green "diamonds". She called it a barrette and said it was a Christmas present from her beau. After admiring it for some time I got up the courage to ask her if I could wear it for a little while. She said I could if I promised "hope to die" that I wouldn't lose it. So I promised and she clamped it into my baby-fine hair. Any proper adult would have known that such fine hair could not possibly sustain a barrette – but I guess my Aunt Jennie wasn't really an adult. More like a very big girl.

When Uncle Arthur arrived he gave each one of the children a handful of silver money and we all sought my mother's permission to spend it at the corner candy store. Permission was granted with the usual caveat about looking both ways before crossing the street and a stern warning that punishment would be severe if anyone even thought about tasting the candy before dinner. We didn't take long over our choices; each child had certain favorites. All the candies were put into one big bag and Ray got to carry it because he was the oldest. As soon as we got home Aunt Jennie came up to me and said she wanted her barrette back and, of course, it wasn't in my hair. Both Ray and Bert accompanied me back to the store, all eyes focused on the ground, but we saw no sign of it. Mr. Miller, the storekeeper, said he hadn't seen it either but he hoped I would have a happy Christmas anyway, and he handed me a large picture card of Santa holding a pipe. I think it was an ad for tobacco. So we all went back home and I told Aunt Jennie that I was very, very sorry and that I would keep trying to find the barrette, and I did.

The rest of the day was taken up with the usual Christmas feast. We all sat at table politely and stuffed ourselves with all sorts of goodies that were only available on feast days. When plates were clean, children were excused to play games while the grown-ups lingered over their beverages and smoked their cigarettes. Mother disappeared upstairs to feed and tend the twins.

It was almost dark when our guests decided to leave. Jennie came close to me, I thought to kiss me good-bye. Instead, she handed me a familiar looking package. It was the little pillow of sachet my mother had helped me to pick out, wrap and label "To Aunt Jennie, with love, from Jean."

"I don't want your present," she said. "I only want my barrette back."

For the first time ever, I was aware that someone had purposely tried to hurt me. Not my body, but something deep inside me. My feelings. I grabbed the package and ran into the kitchen, hoping that no one was looking. After a good cry

I climbed up on a chair, opened the china cabinet, and hid my "shame" behind a large pitcher on the second shelf, the highest one I could reach. As it turned out, my father noticed it that same evening when he was preparing his tea. "What's this?" he said. "Did someone forget something?" I told him my story and as I did so I experienced yet a new sensation: embarrassment.

That awful incident must have "blown over" as the saying goes for I was not aware of carrying it around with me. Aunt Jennie came to all our family feasts and parties and never mentioned the barrette again. We never became close, but Jennie was not the sort of person that one became close with. I left home at an early age and lived in many different states and countries, sometimes not seeing my family for years, but I always sent Christmas messages and Jennie was on my list. She sent cards to me, too, whenever she could remember where I was and what name I was using. This annual correspondence continued until one of my cards was returned. I then learned she had been placed in a nursing home because she was no longer able, either physically or mentally, to cope with the vicissitudes of this life.

Jennie lived to be 87. At the time of her demise I happened to be visiting one of my brothers who lived in a town not far from her last residence. Of course I went to her funeral out of respect and family solidarity, and because I thought it might be interesting to visit with some of my cousins whom I hadn't seen in years. At a certain point in the funeral service the pastor invited the mourners to share their memories of the departed. I never say anything at those times because I am a shy person and have a soft voice, but I always think about what I would like to say if only I could. Happily, I remembered that the year I graduated from high school my aunt took me on a camping trip to Cape Cod and even let me drive her car a short distance along a back road. What a pleasant memory! Sad to say, and I do regret it, I also had a very vivid flashback of the Christmas when I was six and my Aunt Jennie returned my Christmas present because I had lost her barrette.

Day Six

(1937)

*on which she manages to hide the
greatest disappointment of
her entire lifetime*

Great
Expectations

*M*y talent for recalling vivid images and strong emotions ceased abruptly some time during my first year at school. Probably that was just a normal result of my wider horizons: of having become one of the older children in the family, no longer the center of attention. What happened to me, I realized, was just part of what was happening to everyone else. Christmases came and went – some happy, some not so happy – but none impressed themselves upon my memory as those very early ones had done. None, that is, until the Christmas when I was twenty-one.

I came of age during the era now known as The

Great Depression. Millions were out of work, and corporations that employed women hired single women only. When a female employee married, she automatically lost her job. That seemed only fair and logical since husbands were legally responsibly for the support of their wives. (No, I'm not making this up!) But physiological realities do no adapt rapidly to economic conditions, so some compromise had to be found. That compromise was the extended engagement. When young people found their life-companions they became engaged. The engagement ring was the symbol of their intentions. What happened after that was strictly between the engaged couple. It was not unusual for an engagement to continue for four, five, or even more years.

My home at that time was a small, shabby furnished room in the Borough Hall section of Brooklyn. On weekdays, from nine until five, I worked as a clerk for a large insurance company in Manhattan. From six until ten, on Mondays, Wednesdays, and Fridays, I attended classes at New York University. The other two evenings I spent in the university library preparing assignments. On Saturdays I slept late, cleaned my room, washed and ironed my clothes, and did whatever necessary shopping my meager resources permitted. And then – because my professors had made it quite clear that although they could not refuse papers in longhand, all things being equal, a typewritten manuscript would receive a better grade – I boarded a train for the suburban town in New Jersey where my parents lived with the twins. There, after a brief visit over supper, I typed out my assignments on my father's ancient Underwood.

Perhaps that sounds like a pretty full schedule, but there is more. There was a young man with whom I had been going steady (as we said then) for a year and a half. We had met at the university soon after I began attending and were immediately attracted to one another. He was older than I and already had an engineering degree but had decided he wanted to become a doctor. He was attending university to satisfy some pre-med requirements before applying to med school. Our schedules were equally hectic but different. Most of his classes met during the day; his job hours were after midnight and on weekends. Nevertheless, we managed to see each other almost every day, and spent all our free time together. Given our circumstances, the relationship was quite satisfactory for both of us.

On one of the rare occasions when Jack and I had a whole evening to spend together he escorted me to a symphony concert at the Brooklyn Academy. The music was sublime, uplifting.

Mostly Mozart and Schubert. No twentieth century dissonances to contend with. We left the hall in a spirit of elation among a crowd of happy people. As we stood on the curb awaiting a bus to take us to my little room, Jack suddenly grasped my mittened hand, looked into my eyes and whispered, "I have just decided what I am going to give you for Christmas."

Oh, thank you, God, I prayed. I am about to receive the coveted symbol of our intentions, the badge of approval for my lifestyle. Could any young woman be more fulfilled? All I could manage to say was, "Gee, Jack, I don't know WHAT to get you."

December 24 was a half-day at work. Supervisors ordered sandwiches brought in for their crews and then the liquor began to flow. I had experienced one of those office parties the year before and had no wish to participate in this one, since I had learned my tolerance for alcohol was only slightly above zero. Jack promised to pick me up promptly at one, and he did. He had also agreed, for the very first time, to go to New Jersey with me and meet my family. We were expected for Christmas Eve celebration. How we would spend the time between one and our five-twenty departure I had left up to him.

"I'm taking you to the hotel," he said as we climbed into a waiting cab. "I want to give you your Christmas present." The hotel referred to was the gentleman's apartment he shared with his father. I'd been there before. One large twin-bedded room with complete bath and a vault in the wall for valuables; one tastefully appointed sitting room with half-bath for guests. We wished the doorman a Merry Christmas on the way in, embraced in the self-service elevator on the way up. All was right with the world!

When we entered the sitting room Jack insisted that I hide in the guest bathroom while he got out my present. That seemed a bit quirky to me, but hey, who cared? I was cold and shaking with anticipation, said I would like to keep my coat on. I sat down on the commode feeling my heart thump, listening to my ears buzz, aware of my shallow breathing. What's taking so long? I wondered. Maybe he had forgotten the combination to the vault.

Finally I heard his voice. "You can come out now." I pulled myself together, opened the door and stepped into the sitting room. There on a table before me, neatly displayed as in a store window, flecked with simulated snow and decorated with a big red bow, I beheld a Remington, Noiseless, Portable Typewriter.

If only this were fiction, I would stop right

there... but I am committed to a memoir and feel obliged to relate the remainder.

⌣⌣

I hid my disappointment rather well, I think, making much of the fact that the noiseless model was particularly ideal for me because of my sensitivity to noise – a fact he already knew. I asked him for two sheets of paper, one to protect the roller, and when he produced them I rolled them into the machine and exhibited my skill: "Now is the time for all good men..." After my demonstration he illustrated the pick-and-choose method: "Patsy, I love you." We each had a glass of sherry and some Schraffts cookies his father had left for us. We kept our appointment with the five-twenty. We did not take the typewriter.

As the train approached our destination I began to feel nervous. I knew my mother was not going to approve of my companion. With his blue-black hair and neatly trimmed mustache he was much too handsome and sophisticated to be trustworthy. My mother tried very hard to be a good Christian; she knew all God's children were equal, but, for her, His Anglo-Saxon children were just a tad more equal than others. I needn't have worried, though, because despite her many years of ill health, that evening she was the very soul of hospitality. Dinner went smoothly – everyone putting his best foot forward.

After dinner was the time for exchange of gifts. My sister and brother both insisted, "Jean go first", so I led the way to the tree. I quickly saw that the largest package under it had my name on it. Thinking it too large to lift, I sat on the floor and pulled it toward me. First I admired the wrapping, as I was meant to do. Then I untied the ribbon and folded back the tissue. What emerged was unmistakably the carrying case of a Remington Portable Typewriter.

Day Seven

(1942)

true fulfillment at last

"...A Lovely Light"

I was married on my twenty-fifth birthday, in midsummer of 1941. It wasn't the culmination of a long and romantic courtship. A compassionate mutual friend who knew of turmoil in our separate lives believed that we could find solace in each other's company. After a couple of months of dating, we agreed.

Europe was at war and the U.S. had initiated a peacetime conscription; almost all able-bodied young men up to the age of twenty-eight were being drafted into one of the branches of military service. When John proposed he made sure I knew he had passed his twenty-eighth birthday in

June and therefore was free to make a complete commitment.

He moved the contents of his furnished room –mostly clothes, a few books and trophies– into my tiny apartment and we started learning to adjust to each other's ways. John was a particularly creditable housemate. He had grown up on a farm and was handy with tools (a talent none of the men in my family had). When he was thirteen, the oldest of four, his mother died of pneumonia. There being no aunts or grandmothers available, it fell to his lot to do most of the housework and care for his younger brothers. As a consequence he was most appreciative of any little chore I did in his behalf. And in my absence he would do whatever job needed doing regardless of its gender affiliation. Of course, as with any relationship, there were occasional misunderstandings and a few tears, but they were surprisingly few and quickly resolved. It was not long before we realized we had fallen deeply in love and had every reason to look forward to a long and fruitful life together.

Then came December 7th!

We both knew instinctively that within a few months John would be in uniform. We didn't talk about it much. The thought of separation was too painful. We spent as much time together as possible, and were particularly solicitous of each other's wishes. A kind of hush came over our lives, as though we were waiting outside a hospital room where a loved one lay dying. I don't remember anything about our first Christmas together. I suppose we must have done some decorating, sent some greeting cards, exchanged gifts, or feasted in our favorite restaurant. I just cannot recall. Whenever I try what comes to fore is a feeling of excruciating tenderness enveloped in a fathomless fog of doom. In retrospect, I suppose I was suffering a clinical depression.

By the middle of March John was in basic training in South Carolina and the rhythm of my life had returned pretty much to what it had been before I knew him: office work, university classes and study, with little or no recreation.

We wrote each other nightly, as did thousands of other couples who had been separated by the need to train for war. When my two-week vacation came due John found me a furnished room in the town near the base and we were able to spend some time together.

I decided not to register for fall semester classes, thinking there might be an opportunity to see my husband again before he was shipped overseas. The money I had saved for tuition might come in handy for last minute travel. In

October John wrote that he had been promoted to sergeant and given an assignment purported to last at least three months (nothing was ever definite in the Army). He asked if I would be willing to give up my job and join him. I gave my notice the very next day.

We were lucky to find a "chauffeur's" apartment over a large garage behind the home of a local businessman. It was on a Beltway, half way between the base and town, and a bus made the loop every hour during the day, less often in the evening. John's assignment turned out to be a very reasonable one. He was able to join me most evenings for supper and did not have to be back in camp until six in the morning. For the first time in my life I was able to claim Occupation: Housewife.

Most days I would sleep late, have a leisurely bath and breakfast, tidy up the apartment and then ride the bus into town in search of adventure. I thought at first I would have a great deal of time on my hands, but it didn't turn out to be so. Every little project I had in mind, such as buying a new toothbrush or mailing a package, took three to four times as long as I expected. In the deep South, I learned, each transaction must be accompanied by a lengthy conversation in a slow drawl. Any attempt to speed things up was considered hostile. I acquiesced, and with my talent for mimicking was soon sounding like an authentic Carolinian.

Our landlord owned several acres of woodland on the opposite side of the Beltway. On the Sunday before Christmas he told us we were welcome to cut our own tree, and he showed John where he kept his axe and other tools in the garage under our apartment. I was ecstatic! I had never even imagined cutting down one's own tree. In some weird quirky way I still half-believed there was a Santa who did that. John said he had never had a Christmas tree he hadn't cut down himself. It seemed quite normal to him.

Though the day was warm, we donned our jackets for protection against the scratchy branches. We took the axe and a ball of twine, crossed the Beltway and entered the woods in search of the perfect tree. Each time I chose one that seemed just right to me John said it was way too large for our space. The ones he chose seemed too small to me. I wanted one that would touch the ceiling and make me feel small, like the trees from my childhood. After a few such disagreements he simply stated that a tree looks different in the woods from the way it looks in a room, and I would just have to trust his judgment. On the way back I started to mumble about how we would get the tree up the stairs, what we would use to decorate it, etc...

In a tone of exasperation he said he wished I would quit carping, that he would take care of everything – so I did, and he did.

While I prepared dinner in the kitchen I could hear him moving furniture about in our sitting-cum-bed room. Then he hoisted the tree up through our largest window and fixed it in the spot he thought most suitable. When I peeked in I saw that it filled about one-third of the room. After dinner he announced that he had done enough work for one day and he promptly sat down in the easy chair and started to read the paper. When I joined him with my embroidery I became aware of the sweet scent of evergreen that was slowly permeating the room. Christmas had begun.

The next evening he arrived home with a package from the PX which turned out to contain two dozen candles of a size and shape I associated with jack-o-lanterns and power outages. My immediate reaction was – What? How? Impossible! But I wasn't going to "carp"; I would wait and see. After supper he visited the tool room in the garage and came back with tin sheers and a pair of pliers. Next he invaded the broom closet and hauled out our stash of cans-for-Uncle Sam. With an air of assurance he designed and fashioned a gizmo that would hold a candle upright and attach it to a branch of a tree. After testing to be sure the design was right, he made five or six more before retiring.

The following night he speeded up his production, saying he wanted to finish before Christmas Eve. He stayed up way past his usual bedtime and I worried that he might oversleep and miss his bus in the morning. He assured me that soldiers do not oversleep.

Christmas Eve was on a Thursday and by Wednesday night all the candles were in their holders, ready to shine. John let me decide how they should be distributed among the branches. However, some of the places I suggested were unacceptable because they were too dangerous. When he was satisfied that they were all safely placed, we went to bed.

The next day I prepared a special meal and tried to find a way that we could share it in front of the tree, but there just wasn't enough space. Television and its concomitant tables had not yet been invented. We supped in the kitchen, as usual, and when the meal was over and cleared away the ceremony began. John lit the candles, one by one, making sure once more that they were all safely positioned. I turned out all the other lights in the apartment and we sat on the bed, leaning against the wall, basking in the magic glow.

We sat in silence for a long time, just enjoying the beauty of our surroundings. Then John began to talk to me and tell me about his childhood, and about Christmas on the farm. His parents had been immigrants from Lithuania and had brought with them ideas and customs different from the ones they found here. He told me of games he played with his brothers, and tricks they had played on their grandmother. He professed he couldn't sing, but recited for me the Lithuanian words of a song they sang about lighting the candles on the Christmas tree. I wasn't sure if I was really awake or asleep and dreaming, but I felt my mind and my heart opening up and taking in new ideas and new emotions. Oh, what a lovely light!

Day Eight

(1946)

a different kind of happiness

Only God

*T*here were no family gatherings to attend in 1946. Mother's illness had confined her to a wheelchair, my sister and my brothers were busy finding places for themselves in the postwar economy, my husband had given his last full measure. I lived with my posthumous son in a three-room fifth-floor walkup in Greenwich Village. It was his first real Christmas; he'd been but a babe in arms the year before. For anyone who has not experienced the ecstasy of motherhood I must apologize for I cannot find words to explain it. What comes to mind are snatches from the carols: Joy, joy, joy! Oh come let us adore Him... In a more secular mood, I began to ponder the myth of Santa Claus and how it must have originated. Then I understood what my mother had meant when she told me she was my Santa.

We had no fireplace or cubby holes, no private bedrooms like those of my early childhood home, but we were quite comfortable in our space – once the stairs had been navigated. And so far I'd been able to manage our income so that we could spend all of our time together. Now it was up to me to provide the magic of Christmas for this little man-child of mine. Where to begin? Gifts, of course, the Magi brought gifts.

The next few days were fair and not too bitterly cold. When nap time came I bundled up Little John snugly in blankets, strapped him into his stroller, and off we went. While he slept, I visited every toy store, drug store, hardware store, book store, music store, and five-and-dime within walking distance of our apartment – and there were many.

By week's end I had managed to deplete a large portion of my savings, but I was pleased with my purchases. Each gift had been chosen with care for its appropriateness for his age and ability. There were blocks and picture books, mechanical toys, a one-octave piano and a drum, a hand-wound record player with records of the nursery rhymes and one with the story of The Little Engine That Could. And a little piece of canvas cloth cut and stitched in such a way that it fit perfectly over a standard card table to make a tent. All that remained to be done was to transform our living room into a fairyland, like the one my parents had prepared for me so many years ago.

The most important feature, I decided, would be the tree. I hadn't had much experience trimming trees. During my years in New York I had been quite satisfied with the corporate trees in the lobbies of office buildings where I worked and the department stores where I shopped. Who could compete with those? For Little John's first Christmas, though, we must have a large tree that would fill the corner of the living room and dazzle everyone who dared approach it. I knew where trees were being sold (frighteningly expensive!), but how would I ever get one up the stairs? My younger brother, recently discharged from the Marines, was staying with friends in the City while aggressively searching for a job, and a wife. I phoned to ask if he could help with my project.

"I can get you a tree on Saturday," he said, "and I'll carry it up the stairs but I won't be able to stay and help you trim it because I'm leaving at noon for Boston to meet Ginnie's parents." Ginnie was the girl he hoped to marry. He delivered the tree on schedule, placed it on the landing outside my door, out of the line of traffic. To make sure his efforts would not be wasted, he attached a handwritten note – "Property 5S – please do not remove. Santa." I thanked him and wished him good luck with Ginnie's parents, and he was off.

Later that day, while Little John was napping, I propped open the door to my apartment, went out into the hall and approached my tree. First I grabbed it by what I judged to be the top. Wow! Those needles were prickly. I went back for gloves. Then tried to develop a strategy: how best to move this giant? There didn't seem to be any right way. In desperation I started pushing, pulling, kicking, cursing. I even tried reasoning with it. It did, finally, condescend to enter the apartment. The next problem was to attach the stand I had bought which was claimed to fit all trees. Wonder of wonders, it did fit this one. Within a half hour of starting to read the instructions, and with only two bloody knuckles, I had an evergreen standing in the corner of my room. But was it a tree? All the branches grew out of one side, and the top, where the star was meant to go, curled over and looked down, as though heeding the call of gravity. I was exhausted from my efforts and I heard John stirring in the bedroom. There was nothing to do now but put the tree out of my mind and deal with it later.

That evening I called my friend Clare who lived uptown. Clare and I had been best friends in third grade and fourth and fifth, until my parents had had to move because my mother got very sick. Our lives had taken very different turns but every few years our paths would cross and we would pick up where we'd left off. Clare was employed by a large bakery and restaurant chain and had worked her way from waitress to baker and sales person and most recently, because she demonstrated noticeable artistic ability, she had been trained as a window dresser. I thought she might have some suggestions as to what I could do with my tree.

"I know this is your busiest season," I began, apologetically.

"Busy isn't the word. It's crazy. I'm flat out. But I must see you before Christmas. I found a wonderful toy for Little John. He's going to love it. When can we get together?"

"You're the busy one. You say."

"I could come tomorrow after church."

How lucky could I be? "I'll have lunch ready."

We ate in the kitchen, which was right off the hall, so it wasn't until after lunch that Clare came face to face with my evergreen. "Where did you get THAT?" she queried. Not wanting to incriminate my brother, I simply said, "Santa brought it."

"Well, I'll see what I can do. It's a branch you know, not a tree. It's an old trick. If I'd known you intended to buy a tree, I would have warned you. Where are your tools?"

The next half hour I spent hunting and fetching while Clare clipped and sawed, hammered, tied, taped, glued and stapled. I was amazed and delighted with the transformation taking place. Clare, though, was less pleased with the results of her efforts. When she was ready to quit she stood back a pace, placed her hands on her hips, tilted her head to one side and remarked, "You know, Jean, that poet was right. Only God can make a tree." We laughed and started hanging ornaments on the still strangely oriented branches. It was good to be in the company of my childhood friend!

While Clare was showing me the wonderful toy she had bought for John – a fire engine with a siren (I could have done without the siren) – it occurred to me that she might enjoy sharing my son's first Christmas. "Why don't we do the Santa bit now, when he wakes up. Can you stay?" She said she would like that. We quickly brought out the toys I had stashed in the hall closet and arranged them around the room. We set up the card table and stretched the canvas across it to make a tent. When all was ready we started to sing – some songs we had learned in the fifth grade when a visiting music teacher first taught us to harmonize.

When Little John woke I told him Santa had come and brought him some gifts. He approached the living room with excitement but, once there, he was overwhelmed by the profusion of new items cluttering up his usual play area. I thought for a moment he was going to cry. His fright lasted just long enough for me to suffer a pang of guilt. What had I done? In a flash Clare was showing him how the fire engine worked and from then on he played his role charmingly – examining each toy in turn, showing them off, asking for help when needed. When he discovered the tent he decided to place his new toys inside it.

When hunger came we supped on what we could find: a can of corned beef hash and some two-day-old deli cole slaw, washed down with a whole quart of temperance egg nog which I had bought for Christmas Eve. After Clare left I helped my son into his pajamas and asked him to pick out a book for his bedtime story. He brought me the animal book, opened at the middle, where two fat beasts he had never before seen stood glaring at each other across the center fold. On the left HIPPOPOTAMUS, and on the right RHINOCEROS. And that turned out to be his favorite page of his favorite book well into the spring, when he was still trying to pronounce their names correctly without prompting.

Day Nine

(1960)

*on which she learns that one plus
zero equals zero*

Empty Nest

*W*hen John turned two he became eligible to attend a neighborhood nursery school for a few hours each day. I took advantage of that free time to return to university and complete my studies toward a B.A. degree. That accomplished, I began to look for greener pastures. New York City was no place to bring up a child. We moved from place to place as opportunities for work and study became available. Our odyssey took us first to Oregon, then Michigan, then Greece, and on to Illinois. Though we lived frugally, we made many good friends along the way.

During all this time, the gamut of my son's childhood, no matter where we were or what the state of our finances, Christmas was always a lavish affair. I made no attempt to curb my compulsion to recapture the magic of the holiday, its aura of mystery, its element of surprise. We decorated our living quarters, be they ever so humble, with holly and mistletoe, and Santa always brought a large tree for us to trim with tinsel and bright ornaments. We developed a ritual of fancy cookie making, of which John took charge at an early age, demoting me to the clean-up chores. We bought, wrapped and mailed presents to all the many cousins – a new one each year, it seemed. When it came to choosing gifts to put under the tree for John, I fell easy victim to the rapidly growing cult of consumerism so rampant in our culture today. No amount was enough. Whatever the hucksters were hawking seemed desirable and right for my boy. And my boy submitted good naturedly to all these excesses, though with somewhat waning enthusiasm as he approached adolescence.

Those years, the happiest of my life, passed all too quickly. Soon it was time for us to adjust our ways to meet John's changing needs. In consultation with our wisest advisors a consensus was reached that John should attend a boarding school, one with particular characteristics to fit his unique personality. After a careful search one was found which seemed just right. It was in Massachusetts, a thousand miles from where we were living. We went there during Spring vacation to see the campus and meet the Headmaster. We were both convinced we had made the right choice. Luckily, my fall semester started later than his, making it possible for me to drive him there again in September to make sure he was safely installed.

When the holiday season arrived he traveled home alone by rail. I felt so proud as he got off the train neatly dressed in suit and tie and carrying a briefcase. In less than four months he had matured noticeably and developed a good share of self-confidence for a fourteen-year-old. We celebrated Christmas much as we always had. He baked several batches of cookies, much to my pleasure, and also relieved me of the chore of standing in line at the post office to mail the gifts to the cousins. He tried to teach me chess but I was not very adept. He escorted me to a performance of The Nutcracker.

But all that is by way of introduction. The memory I wish to recount took place a year later, during his second year at school. A few days into December I began to feel the spirit of Christmas stirring within me, but was at a loss to imagine what I could prepare that would be pleasing to my very grown-up son. I called him on the phone one Sunday night and asked him what he would like for Christmas.

"Do you really want to know?'

"Of course. You know I will get it if I possibly can."

"Well, what I'd REALLY like is enough money to be able to go home with my roommate. He lives in Washington, D.C."

"Oh, well, if that's what you REALLY want. How much would that be?"

"I don't know. I'll have to find out."

"All right. Send me a letter with his parents' name and address and telephone number and the amount of money you think you will need. If I can manage it, I will send you a check."

"Gee, thanks, Mom. That'll be cool."

"All right. I'll be watching for your letter. Good-bye, dear."

"Bye, Mom."

As I put down the receiver I suddenly went numb all over. It was almost like an out-of-body experience. I saw the room where I was standing as though I were looking down on it from the ceiling – only I wasn't in it. I wasn't anywhere. I didn't exist.

༺༻

When the numbness passed I sat down and started talking to myself aloud. "This is a very good thing that has happened. John has made a friend and is starting off on a life of his own. He is developing independence. That is why you sent him off to school, so he could learn to be his own person – get along without YOU – not be a mama's boy. This is what you want. This is good!"

I kept myself very busy during the days and nights between that evening and Christmas Eve. I participated in all manner of social events I had heretofore eschewed. I decorated my home, but modestly. I purchased a small artificial tree which I placed on a table in the front window. I even went to church on Sundays. I did not tell anyone that John was not coming home, and no one thought to ask. Whenever my situation seemed unbearable, I rehearsed the litany I had invented the night of the call. When the witching hour arrived, about 9 pm on December 24, I'd had enough of the stiff-upper-lip. I closed the blinds, opened a bottle of sherry, put my favorite Pachelbel on the turn-table and sat with my eyes closed, wallowing in self-pity.

Shortly before eleven my phone rang. It had to be John. No one else would call me at that hour.

"Hello"

"Hello, Mother. I'm calling to wish you a happy Christmas."

"Well, thank you, that's very sweet. Are you having a happy Christmas?"

"Hmmm...Not really."

"Why? What's the matter? Where are you?

Are you in Washington? Is anything wrong? Do you need help?" (Wishful thinking!)

"No, no, Don't worry. Everything is fine. We're just not having Christmas, that's all. Because --- well, because --- they're Jewish."

"Oh" (much relief!) "But John, you know the Jewish people have a very nice celebration around this time. It's called Hanukkah. They light candles and sing songs and have a feast. It's going to start in a few days, the 28th I think. That should be interesting for you. I'm sure you'll have a good time."

"Well, o.k., but I don't think so. You don't understand, Mother. They're not RELIGIOUS Jewish. They're just... (long pause) PLAIN Jewish."

Day Ten

(1984)

Aunt Jennie revisited, and then
a clash of cultures

Futon & Tofu

By the time my son was ready for college I had earned my doctorate and thus was prepared for the next step up the professional ladder that would provide the funding for that endeavor. The best opportunities available to me at that time were government posts abroad, and so began another odyssey – only this one I had to make alone. It started in Kabul, Afghanistan and after almost three years in that officially designated "hardship post" I was able to transfer to Lebanon – then known as the Switzerland of the Middle East.

John visited me briefly during his summer recesses and I observed, with unexpressed dismay, his gradual metamorphosis from the well-groomed, well-mannered schoolboy of whom I had been so proud into a full-fledged member of the 60's counter culture. He let his hair grow long, moved into a commune, became a vegetarian, practiced Yoga and spent hours each day in meditation – all perfectly harmless acts, perhaps even beneficial ones, yet ones which made me feel uncomfortable in his presence. There were other, more subtle changes difficult to describe: An all pervasive negativity, a studied boorishness, an apparent delight in things unkempt. So this was what was being learned at college in the USA! Nevertheless, he was passing his studies (just barely) and so at the end of the fourth academic year I took a short leave and flew home in anticipation of attending his graduation exercises. This was particularly important to me since I had never been able to attend any of my own. However, upon arrival I learned from my brother that just the night before John had unexpectedly been offered a free ride to California – an offer he couldn't refuse.

Years passed. We were never completely out of touch, just two people living in completely different worlds with little in common to communicate. When my overseas contract was fulfilled I returned to the States and found lodging in a community near where he was living in hopes of renewing our acquaintance. It was a brash experiment which I pursued for the best part of a year, but it didn't work out for me. I felt more a foreigner in San Francisco than ever I had in Kabul or Beirut. And so, after thirty-odd years of exile, I returned to the Northeast where I belong.

The first few years back home I celebrated Christmases with my siblings and some of the seventeen nieces and nephews with whom they had provided me. Although these young people had seen very little of me while they were growing up, I had become the legendary Aunt Jean who traveled in far off places, and they welcomed me into their hearts and homes as if I had never been away. And then, very late one mid-December evening I received a telephone call from my son inviting me to spend the holiday with him. I was overjoyed and immediately set about arranging transportation. Because of the short notice, I was obliged to accept a schedule with a most inconvenient arrival time. Fortunately, a former colleague who lives just a few miles from the airport was willing to meet me and put me up until a more reasonable hour.

With no time to shop, what gift could I conjure to match such hospitality? Eureka! A recently published book I had just finished reading was the perfect fit. My friend, who had taught English to middle-aged Chinese women, had scores of engaging anecdotes about the thoughts and ideas they were trying to express. The book I had in mind was Amy Tan's "Joy Luck Club", a delightful tale of Chinese-American mothers and daughters. I wrapped it appropriately, intending to place it under her tree to be discovered after I had left. But my friend intercepted me and insisted on opening the package.

"Oh, what a great book – but I've already read it. Take it along with you and give it to someone else. Spread the joy around."

No offense meant, and none taken, I thought... But why then did that little spot somewhere between my heart and my liver keep quivering, exactly as it had done when my Aunt Jennie returned my sachet? Had I not matured emotionally in sixty-two years?

When my son's workday was over he came for me and as we drove along he explained the logistics of my accommodations. The house we were headed for belonged to him (and the mortgagee) but it was temporarily rented to a lady who was studying to be a masseuse. She had agreed to let me occupy the back bedroom, share the bath, and prepare breakfast and snacks in the kitchen when it was not in use. He was living in the garage.

We stopped to eat dinner in a vegetarian restaurant and then continued to our destination. As we entered the side door I noticed that the vestibule was full of shoes so I removed mine and added them to the pile. We went directly to the back bedroom where Hanna was hanging curtains, presumably for my benefit. John introduced us and we greeted each other pleasantly, but not warmly. The room was furnished with one medium-sized pallet or mattress made up with clean sheets and a blanket, and one large, low coffee table. There was a closet but it appeared full. I asked if I might have a small chair or bench to drape my clothes over while I slept. Something was found to suit my purpose. I was exhausted from my trip and went straight to bed.

At first I slept but later I awoke stiff jointed and trembling with cold. I had cramps in my legs and back and shoulders. I felt as though I had been sleeping on a rock or perhaps a block of ice. As soon as I could convince my body to move I got up and put on a sweater, my overcoat, and a pair of wool socks and then lay back down and pulled the blanket over my head. Gradually I warmed up enough to fall off to sleep but the hardness of my resting place played a part in my dreams.

Apparently my bodily functions were still on Eastern Standard Time for I awoke very early. I hesitated to rise for fear of waking Hanna. After what seemed an eternity I heard water splashing and other early morning sounds. Soon it would be my turn, I thought. But then there was conversation and more splashing and after that the unmistakable drone of an electric razor. There was, it seemed, a significant other.

Eventually I heard a heavy door slam and after that silence. I rose, showered and dressed and attempted to put some order into the hard lump that served as my bed but soon decided I was not enough of an acrobat to do a good job, and gave up. I went into the kitchen. It was tidy and clean but there was no sign of food or any note of instructions. I timidly knocked on the garage door but did not rouse my son. I knew from past experience that he liked to sleep late on days off so decided to take care of my own needs. I walked to the corner grocery, bought cereal, milk and instant coffee, returned home and ate breakfast.

What now? It is my custom to pass waiting time in reading but I hadn't thought to buy a paper while I was out and there was no printed matter in sight. I'd finished the book that I'd brought to read on the plane and given it to my seatmate, a woman about my age who was also traveling to spend Christmas with her son. I hadn't been given permission to use the television or radio. I went into the back bedroom, rummaged around in my bag for the gift book my friend had rejected and decided to read it again – only this time in a different order. I would rearrange the chapters so that I could follow each character's story from beginning to end. That would make it easier for my Western linear-oriented mind. Sitting upright on the rickety chair I had requisitioned for my clothes horse, I donned my freshly-wiped reading glasses and began my revision of "The Joy Luck Club."

I was well into my third chapter (Amy's twelfth) when I heard stirring in the kitchen and went in to discover John cooking a pot of oatmeal. He offered me some but I declined. While he ate we discussed how we would spend the rest of the day. He told me we had been invited to the ashram he frequented for supper and evening service. If I agreed to go we would have to leave at four o'clock as it was about a sixty-mile drive. In the meantime we could go for a nice long walk in the sunshine, visit some of the festively decorated shops on Main Street, maybe even buy each other presents. He asked me to remind him to get some little cakes, for he had agreed to contribute a dessert toward the supper.

We are both avid walkers and we did all of the above, much to my pleasure and satisfaction. Primarily, though, we visited pastry shops, inspecting and tasting their different wares. I had no idea a single community could support so many sweetshops. What surprised me most though was that all the proprietors seemed to know my son by name! Eventually we found a shop that had a sufficient supply of a confection he considered suitable. By that time I was quite sated, almost to the verge of feeling ill. But, oh, it had been such a wonderful, wild, silly, carefree way of spending a holiday! Was I really a grown-up?

We went back to the house, freshened up and started out on our journey to the ashram.

It was quite dark when we arrived but I was aware that we were approaching a beautiful large house atop a very high hill and that there were no other buildings in the vicinity. As we entered we stumbled over the inevitable collection of shoes, and I obediently removed mine and reached into my pocket for the woolen socks I had been foresighted enough to bring along. We climbed a rather steep stairway, made a left turn and entered a huge kitchen where several large cauldrons were bubbling away on a gas-fueled cookstove. People – mostly young women in ankle length skirts – were milling around the room, talking intensely. Some were stirring the cauldrons. I became aware of spicy odors: some familiar, some arcane. People began welcoming me and offering juices. John went off to another part of the building to help with some chores. Someone gave a signal and people started picking up bowls and spoons and walking toward the stove. A young couple approached and asked if they could help me. I peeked into the various pots. Many of the offerings were unfamiliar to me and did not look particularly appetizing. I settled for a ladle full of rice and lentils and a wad of deep-green leafy substance. I followed the crowd toward the adjoining room expecting to find a communal table but no such luck. Many of the occupants were still milling around and conversing while they ate. Others sat cross-legged on the floor in groups of three and four. Since I am not adept at eating in either stance I glanced around urgently seeking some more comfortable niche. Directly across from where I stood was a picture window with an extra-wide sill. I wormed my way to it and sat down to consume my meal. After a while someone came by with a dish of the little cakes we had brought and some sweet cardamom tea. I took neither; I'd had sufficient sweets for that day.

When I had cleaned my plate, I returned it to the kitchen and joined the gently flowing crowd through yet another door and into a long cold corridor. There I saw my son walking toward me carrying a folding chair. "Take this," he said, "You may need it. The service is rather long. Some older people need a chair." I felt self-conscious but trusted his judgment.

The room we entered was dimly lit and heavily incensed; a dais occupied one end. It was decorated with flowers and candles and contained a number of framed photographs. One was of a bushy-bearded man – like the picture of God in my mother's Bible. Three were of different women of indecipherable age. The one most prominently displayed, however, was simply a picture of bare feet. I tried to fathom the significance of it but could not. A few supplicants were kneeling on the carpet with hands clasped and eyes closed. Slowly and silently the others filed in and arranged themselves in various kneeling positions. Wishing to participate as fully as possible, I knelt on the carpet too, but kept close to the chair my son had wisely provided.

There was a long period of silence, then a long period of chanting, then more silence. Four young ladies stood up and gracefully walked around the room humming and strewing flower petals. Candles were lit before the photographs. More chanting. More silence. About halfway through I painfully transferred to my chair. I thought it would never end. It did, but not with a grand amen as do most Christian services. Everyone seemed to be in a bit of a trance. Those who lived in the ashram disappeared into the upper regions of the building. Those of us who had come by car let ourselves out quietly so as not to disturb the peace. I was glad there were no prolonged goodbyes, which I hate, but I had a feeling of unfinished business. Once on the road I questioned John about the significance of parts of the service but he had traffic to contend with and was not in a mood for talking.

The next day was Christmas. I awoke to the sound of angry voices. Hanna and David were having an argument in the kitchen. Best to lay low. Check out what Jing-Mei Woo is up to. When the decibels diminished and voices came from another direction I ventured out for breakfast. Hanna stuck her head in the door and asked what John and I were doing to celebrate Christmas. I told her I didn't know. She said that she and David were leaving for his sister's house and would be gone most of the day.

When John emerged from the garage he had a piece of paper in his hand. "I know you like to have a special dinner on Christmas. Turkey is it? A friend of mine helped me make this list of good places that serve your kind of food. I thought we might drive around and look at the posted menus and see what appeals to us. Some of them may serve vegetarian meals as well."

"Wouldn't it be better to telephone? Mightn't we need a reservation?" He didn't think so. His mind was set on reading menus. So be it.

We started out about two-thirty. Almost one-third of the restaurants on his list were closed for the holiday. Those that were open were booked solid and would not even let us in the door. John was visibly shaken; no such problem was within his experience. I was playing it cool but getting mighty hungry as the last bit of daylight disappeared. I suggested, "Why don't we just go to Vegi-Food?" – the tiny, dingy Chinese-Vegetarian restaurant where he took most of his meals. But he desperately wanted to find me a Christmas dinner. We drove up and down dark streets hoping for a miracle.

I was the first to notice it – a fancy scripted neon sign in a store window: *OMNIVORE*. Yes, it was a restaurant. And, yes, it was designed for odd-couples like us. Sorry, the turkey was all gone, but they had some very nice Beef Stroganoff and any number of savory tofu dishes. They served us each a free glass of wine with our dinner. All's well that ends well!

There was no one in the house when we returned. John went into the living room and switched on the TV. We were watching the news when Dave and Hanna arrived. She went into the bathroom; he joined us in front of the tube. When the program finished, he made some provocative remark about one of the news items and suddenly we found ourselves enjoying a very stimulating three-way philosophical discussion.

Just as I was about to make a point Hanna
entered and suggested that John and I go into the
back bedroom so that she and David could have
some privacy. I blew up and said she didn't have
to get so antsy, I was leaving the next morning,
couldn't she manage to be civil for just a few
more hours?

The next morning there was a muffin on my
breakfast plate and a sincere-sounding note of
apology. I didn't deserve it, but I have to admit
I enjoyed the smug feeling that enveloped me as
I read it. I guess there's a lot I don't understand
about communal living.

Day Eleven

(1988)

on which she belatedly begins to
develop compassion

An Embarrassment of Riches

*T*he ensuing years brought a myriad of wedding invitations and announcements of births and baptisms. Although I had settled quite far north of the clan in order to enjoy my retirement in a rural setting, I attended all the celebrations to which I was invited and made a special effort to remember all the new names and faces. It was a pleasant challenge. Lacking grandchildren of my own, I enjoyed sharing those of my siblings. In the back pages of my address book I kept a list of all the newcomers with their dates of arrival and some of their idiosyncrasies as I learned them. That helped me in choosing appropriate presents for birthdays and Christmases.

As the family grew some of the members left for far-off places: Arizona, Alaska, Japan. Others established homes in adjacent states and were sometimes able to get together on holidays. I was often invited by two or more families on the same holiday and since I rather enjoy driving I would rush from one to the other, ending up with two feasts or none depending on my timing.

Unfortunately, even before all the weddings had taken place, some of the marriages began to unravel. And with the unraveling came new relationships, some of which included new small people whose names and birthdates I did not know. At first I tried to fit them into my list in the right order, but it soon got terribly messy and I ran out of pages. It was all very confusing: Families with exchangeable parts, like baseball teams.

I especially remember one Christmas when I was invited by two of my nieces who lived about a hundred miles apart. Since one party was to take place in the evening and the other the next morning, I accepted both invitations – lit a candle to the weatherman and prayed for fair skies. We had all agreed some years back that gifts would be for children only – since there were so many of them. I got out my list and checked with the nieces to make sure they were up to date, then set off for the nearest shopping mall, credit card in hand, to join the holiday frenzy. It was hard work. One set of children had lost an older sister since I'd seen them and gained an older brother. Of the other "family" I knew only the two older boys; the two younger children had been living with their father when last I visited their mother. Anyway, I'd give it a try.

The 24th was cold but sunny; the roads were well plowed. The trip to Connecticut took just under three hours; I made it easily before nightfall. When I parked my car in the spacious back yard, a husky male twelve-year-old whom I didn't know came out to greet me and offered to carry my large box of gifts. Said it was his job. O.K. That was the last I saw of it.

Cindy had prepared a beautiful buffet, to which I added my rum cake and almond cookies. Her husband-of-the-year was manning a small bar in the kitchen. My sister was there with her two unmarried daughters. Also my favorite nephew with the two children from his first marriage. I never did find out where he had left his wife and the new baby. There were lots of people there I didn't know – inlaws and outlaws. They all seemed interested in explaining to me how they fit in. Cindy said we should all eat our fill, there was plenty of food, and afterwards there would be opening of presents.

I remembered "opening of presents" from my childhood. First, and very important, everyone sits down. Then a child chooses a package from under the tree and takes it to a grown-up who reads aloud the writing on the tag: TO (somebody) – FROM (somebody else). The FROM is very important because the TO-person is going to have to thank the FROM-person after the package is opened. (Except in the case where the From-person is far away, like a grandmother in a different country. Then there's a letter to write). The To-person opens the package and holds up the gift for everyone to see and comment on, and then says Thank you, so-and-so, and the whole process begins again. It takes a lot of time but that's what people do on Christmas Eve. At least that's what we did in the 30's and 40's.

The present generation is much more efficient, I learn. (We're now in the 80's). The husky twelve-year-old has done his job well. He has arranged all the packages in piles according to To's. Those children old enough to read can find their own piles; little ones have to ask a grown-up for help. Once you find your pile you start tearing off wrappings as fast as possible. For a while the game seems to be who can make the largest pile of debris in the shortest time. Unwrappers scarcely look at what's unwrapped. It doesn't seem important. Probably isn't. It's just more stuff. They've already got more stuff than they can squeeze into their toy chests. The excitement of Christmas comes from the ripping of ribbons, the tearing of tissue, the bashing of boxes. All hands on, no tools needed. It's a tactile thrill, probably not available any other time of the year. Any number can play.

I left before nine, and was blessed with a full moon and sparse traffic on my drive to the small rural town in upstate New York where my niece Laurie lived with her horses (of prime importance), her second husband, four children; two hers, two theirs and one very large dog. I was shushed at the door because Santa had already been and the children must not be awakened before dawn. DAWN? I'd heard of morning Christmases all my life, but this would be the first time I'd participate in one. Laurie accompanied me to the guest room where we spoke in whispers for a short while and then hugged goodnight.

At dawn, or shortly thereafter, the oldest boy, Shawn, brought a mug of coffee to my room and announced that it was time for presents. Sleepily I put on my robe, dashed some cold water on my face and joined the others in the family room. Indeed, Santa had been! There were many large, expensive, unwrapped and untagged items under the tree that could only be from Him. Things like skis and skates and hiking boots and horse tackle. A barbell with weights. And for the youngest, the only girl, a very fine doll house. Each boy seemed to know which gifts belonged to him, as though he had placed them there himself.

The ceremony certainly lacked the element of surprise I'm accustomed to associating with Christmas, but at least all the children seemed pleased with their loot.

In addition to the gifts from Santa, there were packages wrapped in colored paper, and these were arranged in piles of TO's, just as at Cindy's. That must be the accepted procedure, I thought. I was somewhat embarrassed to be handed a pile of To's for me: professional photographs of the children, an illustrated History of the Hudson Valley, and a lap-desk obviously chosen with my habits in mind. The tags didn't mention who they were from so I thanked my niece, as that seemed to be the proper thing to do. The unwrapping session was much less vigorous than that of the night before, but the unveiled offerings elicited a similar ennui. The big stuff was what Christmas was all about.

As Laurie and I collected the discarded ribbons and papers, the smell of bacon reached our nostrils, and soon Bob called from the kitchen that waffles and maple syrup were waiting. After breakfast my niece accompanied me to my room where we discussed some un-Christmas happenings while I dressed and prepared for departure.

My way home was due East across a mountain peak. It was snowing lightly when I left and my total concentration was on keeping ahead of a storm. When the snow let up and the sky brightened I relaxed and let my mind wander. It was very kind of my nieces, I thought, to include their old auntie in their rituals. It showed they still bore some relic of the old family spirit which was my mother's great strength. They didn't want to think of me alone and sad when others were together and happy. But really, I am not sad when I am alone, and I'm not so sure they are happy. I think their world is a much meaner world than the one I grew up in, and I wish it were not so. I don't believe in prayer but I hope with all my heart that they will find some joy along the way. "Send them good vibes," my son would say. Yes, Laurie and Cindy, I send you good vibes.

Day Twelve

(1990)

on which she accepts things as they are

"Not With A Bang..."

(some items from my diary, with comments)

Tuesday, December 25, 1990

Item: The forecast was for freezing rain but the sun was shining when I awoke so I quickly pulled on my clothes and did my two miles along Kipling Road.

[Doctor's orders. I MUST walk on the days I don't swim. Got to keep those muscles moving so they don't stiffen up on me again. Tuesday is normally a swim day but I figured the "Y" wouldn't be open on Christmas.]

Item: Filled the bird feeders and trimmed the little hemlock down by the pond.

[Trimming a tree now means, for me, hanging

something on it that pleasures the birds. This year it's balls of slightly rendered suet rolled in sunflower seeds. I prefer making strings of dried mulberries, but I wasn't able to find any mulberries this year.]

Item: Called Sloan. Her grandson answered. He told me she'd had a stroke. It was just a small one, he said; they think she will come out of it ok.

When she comes home from the hospital, he'll tell her I called.

[Sloan is Dr. Beatrice Schiller-Sloan, M.D., PhD, retired psychiatrist, former director of a facility for mentally disturbed adolescents. She was my pal and mentor in night school at NYU in the 30's and we've always kept in touch. She's the only person left in the world who calls me Patsy.]

Item: Doty stopped by with some stollen her brother made. He makes it every Christmas from their mother's recipe. Delicious! I asked her to stay but she had other errands.

[Doty is my friend who is helping me learn to play the recorder. We play duets and she is very patient with me. Why can't I learn to read music? I must have tried a dozen times, always with the same results. Is there a special gene for learning to read music?]

<u>Item:</u> Ray called. He got a chuckle out of my silly gift. Things are pretty grim in that household right now, with no let up in sight. Carl won't go to counseling so Joy doesn't either. Ray believes his being there is providential. He feels he's needed.

[Ray is my older brother. He lived on the sea coast of New Jersey for 84 years. Then, after his wife died and he found he couldn't cope, he moved to Pasadena to be with his daughter. That was quite an upheaval for a man who has had two by-passes plus angioplasty. He had barely adjusted to his new surroundings when the 18-year-old daughter of the family was killed in a gruesome automobile accident.]

<u>Item</u>: Made a big pot of vegetable soup and froze it in single-portion servings. It took almost the whole bloody day.

[I HATE to cook, but I like my own cooking.]

<u>Item</u>: Called Clare. Her phone has been disconnected! No other listing for her in Manhattan. How will I find her? I'll have to go to New York.

[Clare is my friend from third grade. She lived in that apartment for over forty years. Whenever I went to New York we had dinner together at the Waverly Inn. I had a birthday card from her in July. Clare always sends me Hallmark cards

that say "To a Special Friend". GOT to find out what happened to Clare.]

<u>Item</u>: Finished up yesterday's puzzle.
[Crossword puzzles are like walks for the mind: some days you enjoy them, some days you don't, but you gotta keep doing 'em so you mind won't rot. Sloan does crossword puzzles.]

<u>Item</u>: Betty called from Audrey's. Most of her grandchildren are there and everyone's fine. She's fretting over the fact that Artie and Tina didn't make it. She assumes that means they're having marital troubles.
[Betty is my sister. She is such a kind, loving, compassionate person that everyone brings her their problems. How ever does she bear the weight?]

<u>Item</u>: Called Ralph to thank him for the video. He's got bronchitis.
[Ralph is an elderly bachelor, former colleague of mine at both Illinois and Beirut. He sent me a video of La Boheme. He gets bronchitis every winter.]

I decided to watch the video. It seemed to me like a nice way to spend the evening. I tried to get Doty to join me and she really wanted to but didn't feel up to driving in the dark. Just as well, too. The promised freezing rain arrived and caused a power outage at the beginning of Act III. I just pulled the plug and went to bed.

<u>Item</u>: John called – about 11:30. He'd been working all day on a computer snafu at Bank of America. He hoped I'd had a merry Christmas.
   [MERRY Christmas?]

Printed in the United States
by Baker & Taylor Publisher Services